Oct 2015

To My Isabella

Love

Annie

The Light We Share

HARRIET R. UCHTDORF

DESERET
BOOK

Salt Lake City, Utah

All photographs and illustrations throughout the book are used by permission. Page 3 xyno/iStock/Thinkstock; page 4 © Irina Schmidt/Shutterstock.com; page 7 © DeZet /Shutterstock.com; page 8 © Agnes Kantaruk/Shutterstock.com; page 11 © col/Shutterstock.com; page 12 © vshtefan/Shutterstock.com; page 15 © Morgenstjerne/Shutterstock.com; page 16 © provided by author (shown at far left); page 18 © lithian/Shutterstock.com; pages 20–21 © greiss design/Shutterstock.com; page 23 © GoodMood Photo/Shutterstock.com; page 24 © JLR Photography/Shutterstock.com; page 27 © Liliya Kulianionak/Shutterstock.com; page 28 jennyhanschen/iStock/Thinkstock; pages 30–31 Carlos Caetano/Shutterstock.com; page 33 Bernice Williams/Shutterstock.com; page 34 © Nailia Schwarz/Shutterstock.com; page 37 © S.Borisov/Shutterstock.com; page 38 © Christian Mueller/Shutterstock.com; page 40 © i-m-a-g-e/Shutterstock.com; page 42 © Peshkova/Shutterstock.com.

Author royalties from this book
will be donated to the
General Missionary Fund.

Library of Congress Cataloging-in-Publication Data

Uchtdorf, Harriet, author.
  The light we share / Harriet Uchtdorf.
      pages cm
  Includes bibliographical references.
  ISBN 978-1-60907-869-0 (hardbound : alk. paper)
  1. Mormons–Conduct of life. 2. Uchtdorf, Harriet. 3. Mormon converts–Germany. I. Title.
  BX8656.U25 2014
  248.4'89332–dc23   2013044876

Printed in Canada
Friesens, Manitoba, Canada

10 9 8 7 6 5 4 3 2 1

IF THERE IS ONE THING WE LEARN AS MEMBERS OF THE LORD'S CHURCH AND AS FOLLOWERS OF THE SAVIOR, IT IS TO BE FLEXIBLE AND TO ADJUST OUR PLANS TO RESPOND TO HIS EXPECTATIONS OF US.

DURING GENERAL CONFERENCE IN OCTOBER 2004, I EVEN HAD TO LEARN NOT TO MAKE ANY MORE DETAILED PLANS FOR THE REST OF MY LIFE.

In 1999 my husband and I had been transferred from Europe to Church headquarters in Salt Lake City. I used to call our assignment in Salt Lake City our "overseas assignment," because I was expecting to go back to our homeland, Germany, back to our children and grandchildren, back to our longtime friends, back to our familiar environment, and back to our home, which we still kept.

It is not that my husband and I weren't used to accepting or adapting to differences. We had learned that

differences can be really fun!

When my husband served in the Europe West Area with fourteen countries and seven languages—all with different cultural backgrounds, histories, food preparations, money, and traditions—we experienced the joy of being with Saints united in the restored gospel of Jesus Christ.

Then came the "transfer" to Church headquarters in Salt Lake City and all of the changes and challenges I already mentioned—including learning to choose the right brand among 75 different kinds of ranch dressings! I also found that in the United States, the salt is saltier, the sugar is sweeter, and the flour needs more liquid. These were facts of life, and I learned to accept them. But I thought these adaptations were just temporary.

In my mind's eye, I can imagine Heavenly Father smiling down at me as I adjusted to living in this new country but continued to make detailed plans for our future, not considering *His* timetable and *His* plans for us.

Then at around noon on the Friday before general conference in October 2004, my husband surprised me with a visit at home. He normally didn't come home for lunch, but he called and said that he could be with me in a few minutes. I quickly prepared a light lunch. When my husband entered our house and he looked into my eyes, he did not say one word, but I could feel in my heart and in my mind that he had been called to the holy apostleship. At that moment, the Spirit bore a strong testimony to me that this was the will of the Lord, and that our lives would be changed forever.

W e spent a very special hour together in our home, sharing our innermost feelings, which included also moments of sacred turmoil. These were tender moments we enjoyed at our wonderful place of refuge and of defense. When he left for his office again, I knew with all my soul that he was truly called to be an Apostle of the Lord Jesus Christ.

Only a few days before, on our daily walk in our neighborhood, we had shared our thoughts that two new Apostles would be called during the upcoming general conference. We were curious who they might be. In our evening prayers, we asked Heavenly Father to bless and protect these new Apostles and their families, and to help them in this great transition. Little did we know or even guess who we were praying for. But I know of the power of prayer, and I know that the prayers of the Saints have blessed us since this change came into our lives.

Alone at home I reflected on my life, our plans, the Lord's plan, and His timetable. My thoughts went back to when I was twelve years old. It was a sad time in my young life. My father had passed away from cancer. He was a great father, a loving husband, just a very good man. He was very educated, spoke five languages, played professionally four different musical instruments in a symphony orchestra, and came from a prominent family of Frankfurt.

My parents had great plans for us. The future had looked bright and promising, even after many destructive years of war. But these two years—terrible years—of my father's illness turned our home into a place of suffering and sadness. After my father's death, my mother was extremely depressed. We went every Sunday to our Protestant church service, but we could not find the balm of Gilead. There was nothing and nobody who could comfort my mother.

Well, not quite!

Our Heavenly Father,
in His great love,
had not forgotten us.

Harriet (at left) with parents and younger sister.

Eight months after the passing of my father, two American missionaries knocked on our door in Frankfurt, Germany. Those two missionaries, guided by the Spirit and well prepared, knew exactly what our little widowed-mother family needed. After a short and pleasant conversation, they handed my mother the Book of Mormon, with some marked verses to be read before their return in a few days. My mother loved to read the Bible, and she was immediately interested in this new book of scripture, curious about its content. When she started to read the Book of Mormon, she could not stop until she had read the whole book. She was so excited about the message that often my sister and I had to sit down and listen as she read to us some verses which impressed her so much that she felt they were just written for her.

Those two inspired missionaries came back after a few days and taught us the plan of salvation. It was like a miracle. Our eyes and hearts were opened to a vision of our earthly existence that until then had been unknown to us. Still, everything felt so familiar. We learned about the purpose of life, where we came from, why we are here, and where we will go after this life. We learned who we truly were—that we were children of our Heavenly Father—and that He loved us and cared for us. They taught us that families could be together forever, even beyond this life.

When these two young men, serving the Lord far away from their own families, testified with power and conviction of this glorious truth, memories came back to me of the last weeks of my father's life and his suffering. I had stood and prayed often at the window of our apartment, looking out to see when the doctor would

come to bring relief for my father's pain. How I loved these two young missionaries, well prepared by the Lord and by their parents, teachers, and friends, teaching us the principles of eternal families. In so many ways, they brought a message of light that relieved our heartache and sadness.

Because of the glorious gospel message these missionaries brought, there was no darkness in our home, because light and darkness cannot occupy the same space at the same time. We felt the Spirit, we knew the message was true, and on this day tears flowed freely and hope came back to our home. This was a true miracle for our family; it was as if angels had been sent to us. Those two missionaries were the angels of glory who brought us the restored gospel.

There is a beautiful hymn of the Restoration which reflects very much how we felt at this time. In some ways, we considered it our "German hymn." We sang it whenever possible, and every time, it touched our hearts deeply. It is a powerful, uplifting, and joyful hymn.

Hark, all ye nations! Hear heaven's voice
Thru ev'ry land that all may rejoice!
Angels of glory shout the refrain:
Truth is restored again!

Oh, how glorious from the throne above
Shines the gospel light of truth and love!
Bright as the sun, this heavenly ray
Lights ev'ry land today.

(*Hymns,* no. 264)

The missionaries invited us to attend church on Sunday. We were a little late and had to squeeze into a filled chapel when the opening hymn was sung. It was exactly this beloved hymn of the Restoration. The members were singing with great enthusiasm and joy. I felt like I was sitting among an angels' choir. I had never heard any of our previous congregations sing with such power and volume.

Today I know this was the first time in my twelve-year-old life that I felt the Spirit of God testifying of the truth of the Restoration. I felt as if I were being wrapped up in a warm and secure blanket of divine love.

The members of the Church welcomed us warmly; they were true friends. We felt immediately part of the family of Saints. We loved to go to church, and we felt at home!

Finally, on a cold winter day, my mother, my nine-year-old sister, and I were baptized, and we stepped through this marvelous gate on our journey from darkness into the light toward eternal life. And we rejoiced, as verse two of this great hymn proclaims:

Searching in darkness, nations have wept;
Watching for dawn, their vigil they've kept.
All now rejoice; the long night is o'er.
Truth is on earth once more!

W e loved our new life. My sister and I couldn't believe how my mother was changing. She smiled again. We talked together, we prayed together, we laughed together. There was that spark back in her eyes, a desire to learn. There was new hope and a joyful heart and face.

My mother radiated what Alma referred to in the precious Book of Mormon when he asked the people of the Church:

"Have ye spiritually been born of God? Have ye received his image in your countenances?" (Alma 5:14).

Yes, she had become a new person!

Such a life-changing decision was not unnoticed by our extended family. My grandmother felt that we had become unfaithful to the faith of our fathers. My Aunt Lisa thought we were out of our minds. She announced that she would search out the missionaries in her town of Gelsenkirchen and convince them of their wrong ways. She found the meetinghouse, she found the missionaries, she talked to them, and she got baptized. It was much more difficult for my grandmother to make this important but huge change in her life. It took many years of watching us and observing how the gospel and the Church influenced our lives before she had a firm testimony of her own and became a member. Now we are all sealed together forever.

I do not mean to make any of this sound as though it was easy or automatic. But over time, and in different ways, the light and truth of the gospel touched the members of our family. Because of it, my life changed forever.

As the blessing of the restored gospel came to our family and to our country, it is now spreading throughout the world. I reflect on an assignment my husband and I had to visit the Saints in Chile and Peru. As we met with the wonderful members and missionaries, the hymn "Hark, All Ye Nations!" was sung in the beautiful Spanish language. Members of various cultural and ethnic backgrounds bore their witness of the restored gospel of Jesus Christ. It touched my heart when a newly baptized, humble brother bore a sincere testimony of the Prophet Joseph Smith in a remote chapel in Peru.

Oh, how glorious from the throne above
Shines the gospel light of truth and love!
Bright as the sun, this heavenly ray
Lights ev'ry land today.

How grateful I am for the many wonderful missionaries—more than ever before—who are serving in all the world today. They are bringing heavenly light into a dark world. As our hymn proclaims:

Chosen by God to serve him below,
To ev'ry land and people we'll go,
Standing for truth with fervent accord,
Teaching his holy word.

My dear brothers and sisters, you are the parents and families who will prepare these young men and women to serve missions. You help them to bring the gospel light to every land today. You serve missions as couples or as mature members and bless the people of the world.

Your influence will be unending as you focus on the strengths of others rather than their weaknesses and mistakes. Our hearts and our eyes should concentrate on the positive things in life and in our fellowman. We are well advised not to wear our noses high in the sky or criticize or judge others. As you share your kind, loving, tolerant, and positive attitude towards life, you will bless your spouses and children and grandchildren, your nieces and nephews and friends, and countless others who feel the radiance of your optimism and testimony.

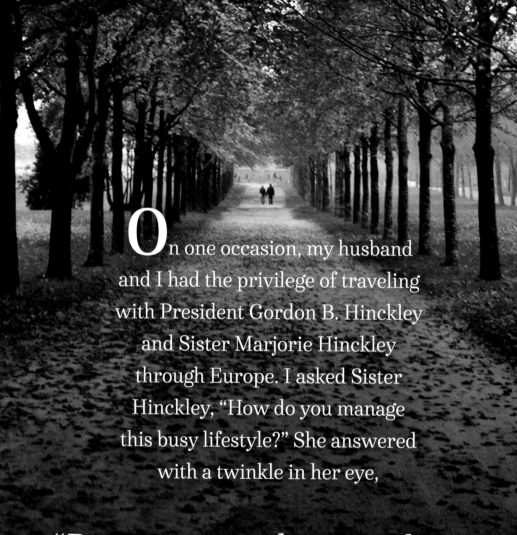

On one occasion, my husband and I had the privilege of traveling with President Gordon B. Hinckley and Sister Marjorie Hinckley through Europe. I asked Sister Hinckley, "How do you manage this busy lifestyle?" She answered with a twinkle in her eye,

"Put on your shoes and go."

How wonderful it is to be motivated
by those who live the gospel with
enthusiasm. This is contagious. And
you, my dear brothers and sisters, are
vibrant and enthusiastic beacons in
an ever-darkening world as you show,
through the way you live your lives,
that the gospel is a joyful message.

You will be an example to our children and youth—an example in decency and quality in everything that affects our lives. You will teach our youth to pray and to study. You will teach them to be confident and have faith in Jesus Christ. You will teach them leadership and humility, and you will help them to claim the gift of discernment through their own righteousness. You will teach them that the truth will not always be popular but that it will always be right. And after all of this, you can promise them:

"That which is of God is light; and he
that receiveth light, and continueth
in God, receiveth more light; and that
light groweth brighter and brighter
until the perfect day"

(DOCTRINE AND COVENANTS 50:24).

My dear brothers and sisters,

thank you for being such a wonderful

influence for good! Thank you for

reflecting and sharing the light of

our Savior, Jesus Christ.

May God bless you and keep you always!